THE HEART THAT KNOWS

IMOGEN WEBBER

ISBN: 979-8-89379-118-1

A gift from the heart, for the heart

Contents

PROLOGUE

I am but a faithful scribe of the whispers of life revealing themselves.

Just as the valley is unveiled through the morning mist, these words gently surrender themselves to me, intoxicating my whole system as they go. Drawing me into the exquisite depths of That which they point to.

My heart, nay my whole being, breaks open again and again to the radical surrender and love of this sacred life.

May these outpourings on these pages draw you into your Self, open you up and wrap around you like a cosy blanket on a crisp, cold autumnal morning.

Listen with your whole being, and you will hear the words that are sung here, deeply in your heart. These are not just poems, they are meditations on the heart and a transmission from the heart, *for* the heart. Each poem, each sentence, each word, each space of silence between, an invitation and a calling.

In love and service,

~ Imogen

There is no teaching

Just a meeting
of the heart
and of the soul
and of the mind

A meeting with our whole being

And in that meeting
the dance of transformation
is known

The seeming separation
is seen
by the heart

As no separation
at all

~

Gently she said

"Let this be included too"

And with that
all the worlds
and all the stars
and all the pains
and all the sorrows
found their home
in the bosom of the heart

The heart that knows

For it knows only this
and this
is love

∾

Come as you are

For all is held

~

Resting as awareness
the dawning recognition comes

I am That

And as That
all is well

All is included

~

Let us sit together under the stars
and share our sorrows and our joys

Let us be reminded that
every sacred human expression
holds such wisdom within it

It is the way in which the Self
comes to know itself
through this painful, beautiful
and heart-opening dance that is life

This is true love
to taste the Self
in all the myriad flavours of existence

May we come to rest in the knowingness
that all that we are
is worthy of this dance

This love

This life

≈

To soften to life
is to sink into
the tender open heart
of curious welcoming

To gaze upon life
with the fresh eyes
of innocence

To surrender
all sense of certainty
and swim courageously
into the Mystery

~

It's all Grace

Some days a fierce Grace to be sure
but Grace nonetheless

~

I rest as I am

The splendour of all that is
fills this heart
full beyond full

There is nothing
that isn't God
the Beloved
the Self

For I am That
and I am all of This

The heart beats
the breath fills this body
with Life's breath

I. AM.

~

We tenderly walk through life
opening further and further to what we find
breathing light into the unlit shadows of existence

This journey of Self discovery
calls us to open to it all

To include it all

∿

To whom shall I bow my head?

For it is all the Self

The Self that has
many faces
many names
many forms
many expressions
many textures
and many tastes

For it is the simple act of bowing
and not to whom I bow
that attention surrenders to

And in this
an emptying-out occurs

I become both nothing
and everything

~

Let us meet
in the depths
of life's great mystery
and drink in the sweet nectar
of the vast unknown

∼

Feel the call of the heart
a call that asks for silence
for rest, for retreat

The call of withdrawal and nourishment
found in the depths of the ocean
in the depths of Being

The soul asks for simplicity
for open-ended beingness

The body calls for rest
for sanctuary

The mind calls for structures and plans left undone
for the unknowing to be welcomed

Wanting nothing
yet welcoming everything

The pain
and the joy
and the sorrow
and the tenderness

All break the heart open further
to the beauty that is
this expression
of life

∽

In the terror and the darkness

I surrender love's dream
and sink through the depths
traversing all manner
of experiencing

I come to rest
in the Self

True love's Being

~

I turn within
again and again

Surrendering
to the inward call
of the open
and unconditional
heart

It asks everything of me
nothing is left out

Yet the heart
gives everything
in return

~

This is the way of the heart

The heart that knows

Where all shadows and shame
all confusions and delusions
are pierced so brilliantly
and yet so tenderly
by the unconditional eyes
of Divine Consciousness

This is the way of the heart

She calls the names
of those that find their feet on this path
and those that dare to listen

This is the way of the heart

∾

The simplicity of being
reveals truth

Can you give yourself
to this simple quest
and be pulled
into the cavernous
depths of being

To be lit
from within

~

I bow before the Altar of Life

With my head touching
the tender ground
of ancient wisdom learnings

My heart cracks open
to the magnitude
of this human experience

My feet firmly planted
in the sacred soils
of the Divine

I bow before the Altar of Life

And give thanks

∼

The Divine exposed tenderly in my heart
the unfathomable revelation

That none of this
is a mistake

∽

There is a cultivation
of continuous attunement
to the hallowed ground of Self

In light of this dawning insight
all other considerations and questions
find their natural resolution

Their rest

Their silence

Their home

～

I invite you into the fire of life
where the light burns so brightly on all that is

The uncomfortable and unfathomable truth
the rawness of this moment
is inescapable and unyielding
leaving no choice but to surrender

The fire burns bright tonight

And with this, the ground shifts beneath my feet

The stability that felt hard won
is gone in an instant
taking with it all sense of knowing
all sense of certainty

My heart burns bright
cracking open with aliveness
to all possibilities

All that is
all that was
all that can be
held in the infinite, fiery embrace
of this moment

Resistance is futile here

There is space for it all
yes, even resistance itself

My heart surrenders
the fever breaks
and with it rushes in a sense of awe and wonder

41

that even this

Yes, even this

Can be included
in this story
of life

~

I do not choose what my soul sings out for

I do not choose how it beckons me

This path that I find myself on
is the path of the heart

And this Way
chooses
me

∾

May this heartbreak
crack you open
and leave
only love
in its wake

~

Seek that by which all else is known

For it is there you will discover
that which you truly are

All questions cease
all seeking quenched
finding oneself in awe and repose
with the perfection of it all

The perfection of this
dancing, ephemeral light show
that we call life

All is included
in the ground of Being

∽

We are held

Through every breath
through every moment
and every happening of life

Even when we can't see or feel that held-ness
through the haze of what we are faced with

We. Are. Held.

~

May you be intimately aware
of the Grace that is holding you

So that you may rest your burdens
at her feet

Let that Grace carry you
in your time of need

Each day at a time

Moment by moment

~

In the emptying out
of personal view
our Divine essence
that we always were
is remembered

It is then
that the dance of the personal
is embraced so wholly
as it is revealed
to be but a facet
of our true Self

Nothing taken away

Nothing added

All a sacred movement
of consciousness
dancing with Itself

≈

Drink in the entirety of this moment
with the innocent eyes
of ineffable knowingness

We open ourselves
to the magnitude and majesty
of this miracle that is life

~

These words are an outpouring of the heart
emanations of Grace

These actions are the movements of life
flowing like a river to the ocean

These sensations are vibrations of the Divine
swimming in its own love

These questions are the clarity of knowingness
pointing back to its silent Self

These emotions are the waves of experiencing
guiding us home

These 'others' are mirrors and reflections
of our very own Being

All is the Self

Without exception

∽

Slow right down
slower than slow

Listen
to the breath
of life

As it emerges

∼

Stilled in the vastness of Being

I feel the great aliveness of This

~

When the thin veneer of control
cracks open and is found wanting

We finally recognise the truth
that there is no free will, not truly

This, when taken hold of in the mind
brings utter horror and fear

But when sunken into in the heart
we find such a sweet taste of freedom

It is a dance of the two to be sure
until the head finds repose in the heart

~

There is no part of us
that is not the sacred upswelling
of Love

~

The veiled
is unveiled

The breath catches
and a sinking
happens
into a repose
with life

What magnificence
this Divine remembrance is
of our wholly sacred
existence

∿

Being tenderly and consciously open
to inhabiting the present moment
and whatever that may bring

A simplicity and freedom can be found
that is intimate, unfiltered and inclusive

Oh how life blossoms from there!

～

Allow yourself to drop deeply
into the present moment

Sinking deeper into yourself
with every breath

All emotions – welcomed
all sensations – welcomed
all thoughts and feelings – welcomed

Nothing to grasp onto
just welcomed without condition

Tenderly
Lovingly
Curiously

Held

～

True love goes beyond
all reasons, all whys
all logical explanations
both for or against

No explanation is necessary

Love just simply IS

∼

When we surrender to life
the recognition arises
that even the efforts
brought about by apparent personal will
are the movements of Grace too

A seed planted in the heart
that we claimed as our own
through misunderstanding

In this way
even doing
is an act of surrender
when it's seen
that there is no doer

Just life playing as life does
through us
as this embodiment
of Self

∾

Forgiveness bottoms out
in the recognition
that there's nothing to forgive

All is
as it needs to be

~

Utterly, deeply
and wholeheartedly
committed

Yet

Utterly, deeply
and wholeheartedly
unattached

This is the way
of the Divine Heart

~

Can we treat every moment as a sacred moment?

Every breath as a sacred breath

Every interaction as a sacred interaction

Every smell, every sound, every sensation

Even every thought

All a sacred expression
of Self, of God, of the Divine

What if it were all sacred?

How would we relate to life then?

∾

Beneath all the veils of conditioning

There you Are

~

Together we dance in the light of the Divine
revealing our nature as none other than That

The tender green shoots of recognition
grow into the mighty oak of realisation

And our beating heart
awakens to the truth

That all is Love

∽

Blessed are those that have emptied themselves
into the heart with reckless abandon

To live from the heart is to include it all
divine and human, infinite and finite
unending and fleeting, formless and form
silence and dynamism

To live from the heart is to meet all that you are
and dance with it until the rising dawn of change

To feel the ground beneath your toes
and the heavens in your vastness

To pour yourself entirely
into every crack and crevice of experiencing

To live from the heart is to live
in the raw unfiltered is-ness of life

To inhabit this moment in all its beauty and pain
without any reference to shoulds or shouldn'ts

∾

The breath of the morning dawn rises gently

Its light permeating the shadows
showing the danger of the dark night to be not

In the dawning light
clarity brings afresh
the realisation that all is well
the realisation that all has its place
the realisation that all is held

In the dawning light
the heart and palms open
to include all

∾

Find your deeper ground

Live from there

~

The great mystery
that is this life

The mind grapples with this endlessly
always wanting to land
somewhere solid
somewhere certain

When we surrender our head into our heart
abandoning its need to be primary and in charge
the mystery takes over

The mystery that has plentiful room
for the desperate clamberings
of the mind and its need to alight

To yield to the unending freefall of the sacred heart
which then becomes your true master

It is found to be a kind and gentle holding

Patient and unconditional
in its endless inclusion of it all

Let your heart become your anchor point
your orientation

Let the Mystery
take hold

∼

Take refuge in the heart

She calls your name
like a siren in the night

Calling you Home

~

There is an utter deliciousness
of this ephemeral
earthly human experience

Light in human form

This is our calling
to savour
the most sacred taste
our humanity

❧

All must be included
into the light of awareness

So that we may flow
unimpeded through and as all of life

Healing the bonds broken
the wounds left raw
and strengthening
the threads of love and peace

Bringing all into a place of rest
a place where all is included
and all is held

So that we may embody
the full potential that we are

Individually
Collectively
Cosmically

All

∼

Listen without prejudice
to life's whisper of inspiration
in your heart

~

Make peace with the present moment
for there is no past and no future

Just This

The Is-ness of life
as it stands

Let this moment
into your heart fully

Breathe it in

Let the gravity
and the magnitude of now
swallow you up
and hold you in her arms

Rest

There is nowhere else to be
nothing else to do

Make peace with the present moment

~

Sinking into the willingness
to be nothing

You discover that you are
in fact

Everything

~

Turn within
again and again
soften and deepen
into the felt vibration
of whatever is arising

Bring everything
into the intimacy
of the moment

Exclude nothing

∼

Empty yourself
of all wanting and needing
all clinging and aversion

Empty yourself
of the need for this moment
to look a particular way

And you will know God
you will know the Self

That knows the inclusion
of it all

That knows the reverence
and acknowledgement
of the preciousness
of the fleeting

In this
you will come to see
that which is omnipresent
that which is stable and continuous
regardless of change

∾

Look beyond the surface
and see the light in the heart
of each and everyone

∾

Welcome it all

The terror, the grief
the resistance, the heartbreak

Let the endless cycle
of shame and rejection
end with you

In the tenderness of your heart
welcome it all

Let all these flavours
and tastes
and textures of life
that have been so
utterly rejected
time and time again

Find their home

In the bosom
of your love

❧

I welcome you into the Heart of Being
where love knows no bounds

Where all that you are
finds its home

Where all that you seek
is discovered to be
what you are

In this place
we remember
that we never left

~

May the heart envelop
with utter tenderness
the mind that needs
to know

~

Surrender, surrender, surrender

All is eaten up
all is included
when we surrender
so utterly to life
in all its forms

Surrender, surrender, surrender

To the heart
that breaks open

Love rushes through

Surrender, surrender, surrender

Even our notions
of surrendering
or not

What we are left with
when all else falls away

Everything

And yet …

Nothing other
than the Self

∾

Can we surrender to resistance too?

To fall in love
with the no
that sings
in the depths
of its walls

~

The melody of loneliness
sings brightly
calling us home
through its voice
and into the heart
of Self

Where aloneness is met
in Love

~

As we surrender into the great unknown
we alight into the deeper ground
of ourselves

Merging so deeply
with the beating heart
of existence

That oh so tender
and yet
oh so ineffable
pregnant home of being

As it is becoming

∽

Purpose?

What could be a more meaningful purpose
than the entirety of creation
unfolding before us in this very moment?

The Divine dancing
its most splendid dance

Revealing itself
to be the kaleidoscopic light show
that it is

All of life
brought to bear
all of you and
all of this

How magnificent!

～

Intoxicated by life

All of existence
is met
utterly
unashamedly

I am drunk on love

❧

Immerse yourself in the deep listening of life

Be lost to everything but this
again and again and again

The unending pull deeper and deeper
into the depths of yourself
the ground of being

The symphony of aliveness that is

Oh the immeasurable vastness of experiencing!

～

Where is the ground of being?

That very sense of existence

Am I not that?

～

Let yourself be entirely pulled
into this moment

Surrender your fight with life
and discover the sweet, causeless joy
of existence itself

Every breath
every movement
every taste

A fleeting, sacred expression of Self

∽

Surrender it all to love

The burden and the pain
the confusion and the fear
the desire and the wound
the heartbreak and the sorrow
the resistance and the contraction
give it all to love

Let yourself be emptied
by this moment

Let it all be included
into the light that you are
the love that you are

Let love fill your heart
with this moment

～

Patience my dear

Let wisdom emerge and blossom
from within

The seeds of clarity
are planted in the heart

We need only to bear witness
to this great unfolding

Timing is everything

∾

In meeting all of you with all of me

Only love remains

~

Resting in the infinite embrace
of the heart

Attending to this moment
slowly, softly
without condition

The opening of the heart

From the heart

To the heart

∼

I am absorbed
into the radiant splendour of Being
and only this remains

Abandoning foolish notions
of I and God
of darkness and light
of form and formlessness

For I am this
and this is everything

Yet words are of no use
as what I am
remains too ineffable
to utter

So instead
I swoon back into
the radiant absorption
of Being

Whence I came

∾

Our eyes meet
the me dissolves
the you dissolves
the we dissolves
only Self remains

Just this

∾

I welcome my lessons
my burdens and my gifts
my pains and my joys
into this grace-filled
moment of life

All that I walk through
is in service to Thee

All that I struggle with
is in service to Thee

All that I achieve
is in service to Thee

All that I am
is in service to Thee

I am Thee

My heart cracks open
my head bows to the ground
and it is revealed

That while I was never truly lost

I am truly
deeply
and wholly

Found

~

There is a vast and causeless joy
in which all is contained
so wholly

~

It's all Grace

All efforting
of practice
of prayer
of doing
of striving
of willing
is but a sign
of the seed of Grace
planted firmly
in the heart

≈

Bow to this moment
letting your head touch
the feet of Life

Surrendering all else
the heart fills
with the sacred fragrance
of the Divine

∽

In the quietude of the heart

There is a radiant absorption

~

I have neither
bounteous breath
nor ample word
to convey
the magnitude
of beauty
that is
this life

~

May you alight
in the wondrous recognition
of your true nature

That surpasses
all comprehension

Where your humanness
is no longer cast aside
with such contempt

As your Being embraces
all manner
of fragrant experiences
meant for the Soul

~

Surrendered into the heart of being

All notions of will
superseded by the remembrance
and the fragrance
of Grace dancing among us

How could it be any other way?

∾

This anger is my temple

This sadness too

All built in the fire of the belly
with every life-force breath
in and out

~

The song of life fills
the sacred ground of my being

Inspiration ignites in my heart

The poignance of this fleeting moment
shall not be lost to me

Instead savoured and tasted
so tenderly and wholly

Oh what beauty is known
through this unimaginable
and unfathomable
dance that is this life

～

Only in the silence
can the fullness of what is pointed to
be heard

Only in the silence
can what is spoken
become what is known

Only in the silence

～

The winds carry the whispers
of the mysteries of life

Listen at your peril
as you may well be taken over
by their utterances of infinite splendour
and expressions too numerous to tell

A song so ancient
so ineffable
yet so entirely known
in the heart of the heart
and the gut of the guts

These winds speak of divine love

They speak of the wondrous grace
that brings us to this moment

But most of all they speak
of the utter mystery
at the heart of it all

~

This sacred space of the heart
guard it with all you have

For it is there that we can know
the truth of ourselves

∼

The Being is Becoming

The tender first flourishes
of consciousness
in motion

What is becoming?

Life

~

In the quietude of being
an absorption, a radiance
an overwhelming remembrance
of what and who I am
is immersively discovered and known

To let go fully into this
is to both disappear
and come into full being
full aliveness

To courageously let go
of the tendrils of the person
is to be reborn
as the universal light
and life that I am
the love that I am

Let go and disappear

In that disappearing
I am found

For what I am is all of this

This that we call life
this that we know
and touch and feel and think

I am it all

I am Consciousness

~

Abandon all the labels
and concepts
and reference points

Live in the direct and unfiltered
being-with-life

A freefall into the Mystery

~

It is in the silence
that the pregnant aliveness
of Grace
is known

It is in the silence
where the spirit can breathe

It is in the silence
where I
am found

~

If we stop running
just for a moment
the very thing
we think we are seeking
is found right here
right now

The alchemy of sinking into
a surrender of the fight
brings us to such depths of being
that all is transmuted in its wake

It is quite a beautiful thing to behold

Reality as we know it crumbles
and what we are left with
is the raw unfiltered
aliveness of consciousness
endlessly playing its complex symphony
of experiencing

Nothing added
and nothing taken away

Yet all a sacred light show
of existence

It is here
where we discover
who and what
we truly are

❧

We are the perfect symphony
of what must be

Let yourself sink
into the recognition
of this

And you will find
that every note
guides you back to Self

Every experience
reveals the light
that you are

~

I bow to Life

Thank you
Thank you
Thank you
Thank you

I lay it at your feet

All. Of. It.

And I bow to Life

∾

About the Author

Imogen is a mystic, writer and mentor who supports those on the path of embodied spiritual awakening. A long-time practitioner of Transcendental Meditation and later a student of various non-duality teachings, in 2015 she experienced a profound and abiding shift in consciousness. She now offers guidance and Divine Light Transmissions, both in 1-1 settings as well as group Satsangs and retreats. Imogen helps people connect with their divine essence and integrate and embody all aspects of their humanness through the unconditional and tender inclusion of it all.

～

For more information:
BeyondImogen.com